MW00915958

to my husband,

By Eden Willow

to my husband, Copyright © 2024 By Eden Willow.
All rights reserved.
No part of this publication may be reproduced, distributed, or transmitted in any
form or by any means, including photocopying, recording, or other electronic or
mechanical methods, without the prior written permission of the publisher, except in
the case of brief quotations embodied in critical reviews and certain other non-
commercial uses permitted by copyright law.

introduction

this book is written for you.

my rock, my soulmate, my incredible husband.

you're not just my partner in life, but also the sharer of my dreams, joys, and challenges.

my love for you goes beyond words, and for the next 100 days, i want you to wake up to a little bit of love each morning.

each page is a daily dose of affection, an uplifting source of encouragement, and a gentle reminder of the unwavering strength of our bond.

you're truly one in a million, and i never want you to forget what an extraordinary person you are and how much you mean to me.

with all my love,

to my husband

DAY #*1*

the way you see the world, full of wonder and excitement, has taught me to cherish every moment.

your joy is infectious and it makes every day an adventure.

to my husband

DAY #2

in the quiet moments when the world seems too loud, i want you to remember that i'm here, always ready to listen, to hold you, to offer a shoulder.

your strength in facing life's storms amazes me every day, but remember, it's okay to seek shelter in my arms.

to my husband

DAY #3

in the quiet moments, i find myself reflecting on how lucky i am to have you.

you've turned ordinary days into extraordinary memories, simply by being you.

to my husband

DAY #4

i admire how you always put our family first, no matter how busy you are.

your unwavering commitment and love for us is the foundation of our happiness.

you're not just a wonderful husband; you're the heart of our home.

to my husband

DAY #5

together, we've laughed, we've danced, and we've lived joyfully.

every second spent with you is a treasure that i hold close to my heart.

to my husband

DAY #6

we've built a life filled with stories, each one a testament to the strength and beauty of our bond.

i am so grateful for every chapter we've written together.

to my husband

DAY #7

in you, i've found more than just a husband; i've found a true partner in every sense of the word.

our teamwork makes every challenge manageable and every joy magnified.

to my husband

DAY #8

every time i look at you, my heart skips a beat.

every shared laugh, every secret whispered, it's all a reminder of
the deep love that has grown between us.

to my husband

DAY #9

i love how you never lose sight of what truly matters.

your ability to balance ambition with compassion and love is extraordinary.

you're not just achieving your dreams; you're making the world a better place along the way.

to my husband

DAY #10

it's in the way you bravely face each day, even when the odds seem stacked against you, that i find my greatest source of pride.

i'm here, not just to walk beside you, but to lift you up when you need it most.

to my husband

DAY #*11*

every dream i have for the future has you in it.

with you by my side, i believe anything is possible.

to my husband

DAY #*12*

together, we've built a life that is uniquely ours, full of love, laughter, and unbreakable bonds.

i wouldn't have it any other way.

you are my teammate in life's greatest adventure.

to my husband

DAY #*13*

you're my first thought in the morning and my last at night.

in the quiet moments, in the chaos, your love is my constant, my north star.

to my husband

DAY #*14*

every step you take, no matter how small, is a victory.

your strength and resilience light up the darkest days.

remember, in my eyes, you are nothing short of a hero.

to my husband

DAY #15

your unwavering trust in me is the cornerstone of our bond.

it's a gift i cherish every day, and i'm constantly in awe of the respect we share.

you make me feel safe and valued, a rare and precious feeling.

to my husband

DAY #*16*

your dedication and hard work never cease to amaze me.

you are the embodiment of strength and perseverance.

remember, in my heart, you are always a champion.

to my husband

DAY *#17*

being with you feels like coming home.

a place where love, laughter, and warmth fill every corner.

you're the heart of my heart.

to my husband

DAY #*18*

with you, every moment is a reason to smile.

your love fills my life with happiness and every day with you
feels like a celebration of us.

to my husband

DAY *#19*

your sense of humor is my constant source of joy.

thank you for making me laugh, for lifting my spirits, and for always finding a way to make the world a brighter place.

to my husband

DAY #20

the respect we have for each other is the melody to our song,
the trust, the harmony.

together, they create a symphony of love that resonates in every
corner of my heart.

to my husband

DAY #21

in your arms, i've found a love that speaks without words, a bond that goes beyond the physical, touching the very essence of who i am.

to my husband

DAY #22

your strength complements mine in ways i never imagined.

together, we are a formidable team, navigating life's journey with grace and love.

to my husband

DAY #23

your kindness is a beacon that guides me through my darkest
days.

your gentle words and thoughtful actions show me love in its
truest form.

to my husband

DAY *#24*

the way you look at me still gives me butterflies.

it's in these small, silent moments that i'm reminded of the depth of our connection.

to my husband

DAY #25

watching you pursue your passions with such focus and
dedication is awe-inspiring.

you have this incredible talent and work ethic that turns every
vision into reality.

your achievements are a testament to your character, and i
couldn't be prouder.

to my husband

DAY *#26*

every challenge we face, we face together, and it's in those
moments i'm reminded of the strength of our partnership.

we are an unstoppable team, and i am so grateful for that every
single day.

to my husband

DAY #27

your heart has a way of understanding things that words
sometimes can't convey.

when you're feeling overwhelmed, remember that i'm here to
share the load, to offer a smile, a hug, or just a quiet presence.

you're never alone.

to my husband

DAY #28

your courage in facing life's hurdles amazes me every day.

you have the heart of a lion and the gentleness of a dove.

never forget, you are capable of achieving the impossible.

to my husband

DAY #29

your laughter is my favorite sound, and your smile, my greatest joy.

the way you light up a room and lift everyone's spirits, it's nothing short of magical.

you have this incredible ability to make everything better, just by being you.

to my husband

DAY #*30*

our dreams are not just fleeting thoughts; they are the seeds of
our future joy.

together, we can nurture them and watch as they bloom into
the beautiful reality of our life together.

to my husband

DAY #*31*

every morning when i wake up next to you, i am filled with a sense of wonder about what new adventures we will embark on.

with every sunrise, our story gets a little richer, and our bond grows a little stronger.

to my husband

DAY #32

every day with you is a new adventure and i wouldn't have it any other way.

your laughter fills our home, your strength supports our dreams, and your love makes everything brighter.

to my husband

DAY #33

in your eyes, i see the fire of determination.

your strength and resilience are the pillars of our life together.

keep shining, for your light leads the way.

to my husband

DAY #34

with every challenge we face, you show incredible resilience and wisdom.

i admire your strength and am grateful for the security and stability you bring to our lives.

to my husband

DAY #35

your happiness is my happiness, and every time you smile, my
world becomes a little bit brighter.

you are the reason for my joy.

to my husband

DAY #*36*

your respect for me shines in your actions, your trust, in your eyes.

it's a quiet, steady flame that warms my soul, lighting our path together.

to my husband

DAY #37

we stand together, united in love and purpose.

our partnership has been my rock, my safe haven in every storm.

with you, every challenge is an opportunity to grow stronger together.

to my husband

DAY *#38*

the sound of your laughter is my favourite melody, a tune that echoes through the best times of my life.

it's the soundtrack of our shared happiness and countless memories.

to my husband

DAY #39

i look forward to every moment with you, knowing that each
day is another page in our beautiful story.

with you, the future is not just bright; it's dazzling.

to my husband

DAY #40

your love lights up the darkest of my days, like a beacon guiding me home.

with you, every challenge seems conquerable, every dream within reach.

to my husband

DAY *#41*

even on your darkest days, remember that you are my light.

i am here to remind you of your strength, to hold your hand through every challenge.

in your vulnerability, i find immeasurable strength.

to my husband

DAY *#42*

i trust you, not just with my thoughts and dreams, but with my
silence and fears.

in that trust, i find a respect that transcends words, a bond
that's unbreakable.

to my husband

DAY #43

your laughter is my favorite sound, it's the melody that soothes
my soul.

in your arms, i find the joy that i never knew i was missing.

to my husband

DAY *#44*

as we walk through life, hand in hand, i can't help but feel that every step we've taken was leading us to this moment.

our past, a beautiful prelude to a love that continues to grow.

to my husband

DAY #45

the future is a canvas, and our love the brush.

every moment with you paints a vibrant stroke, creating a masterpiece that is our life.

to my husband

DAY #46

your smile has the power to light up my world and chase away any clouds.

it's a reminder of the joy and love we share, a symbol of our unbreakable bond.

to my husband

DAY *#47*

in the stillness of the night, i find myself grateful for your presence in my life.

you are my rock, my partner, my confidant, and my best friend.

to my husband

DAY #48

your smile has the power to light up my darkest days.

it's your unwavering support and love that have made our life together an adventure worth every step.

to my husband

DAY *#49*

the way you rise after every fall is a testament to your strength.

your resilience is a beacon of hope in our journey.

together, there's nothing we can't face.

to my husband

DAY #50

we've weathered storms and basked in sunshine, always
together.

i am excited for all the adventures that await us, hand in hand,
heart in heart.

to my husband

DAY #51

every day, i find something new to admire about you.

your strength, your kindness, the way you tackle challenges with such grace.

you're not just my partner, you're my hero in so many ways.

to my husband

DAY #52

your love is like a warm blanket on a cold night, enveloping me
in comfort and security.

you're the peace i've always yearned for.

to my husband

DAY #53

in your eyes, i find a trust that never falters, a respect that never wanes.

it's in the way you listen, the way you understand, that tells me i'm home.

you are the haven of trust i always dreamed of.

to my husband

DAY #54

in every shared sunset, in every whispered dream, in the quiet
moments before sleep, i find myself falling in love with you all
over again.

to my husband

DAY #55

i love how you love me, completely, unconditionally.

it's in the little things, the everyday moments, that your love shines the brightest.

to my husband

DAY #56

our journey together has been filled with laughter and joy,
memories i cherish deeply.

your sense of humor and your warm smile make every day
brighter.

to my husband

DAY #57

life with you is an endless summer, full of bright moments and warm smiles.

you are the joy that lights up my life, now and always.

to my husband

DAY #58

looking back at all we have experienced together, i am filled with gratitude.

each challenge and triumph has woven a richer tapestry of our love.

to my husband

DAY #59

you have an amazing ability to turn the mundane into magic.

your creativity and passion for life inspire me every day, and i am so grateful to be on this journey with you.

to my husband

DAY #60

you tackle life's challenges with such grace and fortitude.

your strength is a source of endless inspiration.

together, we are an unstoppable force.

to my husband

DAY #61

through every hurdle, every setback, i've watched you rise, stronger and more resilient.

but remember, in moments of weakness, my strength is yours.

together, we are unbreakable.

to my husband

DAY #*62*

every time i look at you, i am reminded of our journey together,
the laughter, the tears, and every little moment in between.

it's in these everyday experiences where i find the true essence
of our love.

to my husband

DAY #63

your unwavering spirit in the face of adversity is nothing short of remarkable.

you turn challenges into stepping stones.

remember, with you, every dream seems attainable.

to my husband

DAY *#64*

your resilience in the face of adversity is my daily inspiration.

your strength is the foundation of our shared dreams.

remember, with your spirit, we can reach the stars.

to my husband

DAY #65

remember, it's okay to let your guard down with me.

in your moments of doubt, i'll be the mirror reflecting your
inner light, the one that never dims, even when times are tough.

to my husband

DAY #*66*

your resilience astounds me.

through every challenge, you emerge stronger and more
determined.

i am in awe of your courage and the quiet dignity with which
you face life's ups and downs.

to my husband

DAY #67

with every beat of my heart, i love you more.

you're not just my partner; you're the other half of my soul, the rhythm to my life's song.

to my husband

DAY #68

every day with you is a lesson in true teamwork.

i love how we tackle life's challenges together, always finding
strength in our unity.

our partnership is the foundation of everything beautiful in our
life.

to my husband

DAY #69

every step we take together is built on the solid ground of
mutual respect and trust.

you've shown me what it means to be truly understood and
valued.

your faith in me lifts me higher, and i'm forever grateful.

to my husband

DAY #70

seeing you tackle each day with such grace and determination fills me with awe.

you make the impossible seem possible.

your strength is my guiding light.

to my husband

DAY #*71*

from the highs to the lows, we've navigated this journey hand in hand.

your support and unwavering partnership mean the world to me.

we are more than just a couple; we are a team.

to my husband

DAY #72

you're the epitome of integrity and grace.

the way you handle success with humility and setbacks with a
calm resolve is something i deeply admire.

you inspire me to be a better person every day.

to my husband

DAY #*73*

thank you for always believing in me, even when i struggle to believe in myself.

your unwavering support is my greatest treasure.

to my husband

DAY #74

your trust is my guiding star, your respect, my anchor.

together, they navigate me through life's storms to the calm
seas of your love.

to my husband

DAY #75

finding someone who respects you as an equal and trusts you
implicitly is a rare gift.

in you, i've found that and so much more.

you're my rock, my peace, my heart.

to my husband

DAY #76

you are my confidant, my supporter, and my partner in every adventure.

together, there's nothing we can't face.

i cherish our bond of teamwork and love.

to my husband

DAY #77

in your eyes, i see the kindness and wisdom of a thousand
lifetimes.

you have this gentle strength that reassures me, no matter what
life throws our way.

you're not just my rock; you're my guiding star.

to my husband

DAY #78

life with you is a beautiful collaboration, a blend of your
strengths with mine.

our partnership is my most treasured gift, and i'm grateful for it
every day.

to my husband

DAY #79

with every step we take together, our path brightens.

the future holds so many promises, and with you, each one feels within reach.

to my husband

DAY #80

do you remember the first time we danced under the stars?

it feels like a lifetime ago, yet as fresh as yesterday in my heart.

those moments with you are the treasures i hold closest.

to my husband

DAY *#81*

in this complex tapestry of life, you are the brightest thread.

your spirit and determination inspire me to be better.

together, we can conquer any challenge that comes our way.

to my husband

DAY *#82*

our journey hasn't always been easy, but it has been ours, and that makes every challenge worth it.

your resilience and love are the cornerstones of our shared history.

to my husband

DAY #83

you have this amazing ability to see the good in everyone and everything.

it's one of the many things i adore about you.

your positivity and warmth are contagious, and i am so grateful to have you in my life.

to my husband

DAY #84

our life together is like a beautiful dance, full of rhythm and harmony.

i love how we move together through each day, supporting and lifting each other up.

to my husband

DAY *#85*

in your eyes, i see a future filled with laughter, love, and endless possibilities.

with you, every step feels like a new beginning.

to my husband

DAY #86

in the tapestry of our lives, each thread you weave is filled with love, strength, and kindness.

you've made our life a masterpiece of love.

to my husband

DAY #87

in your eyes, i find a happiness that words can't describe.

your love is the light that guides me to true joy, every single day.

to my husband

DAY #88

life can be a turbulent sea, but together, we've weathered every storm.

know that i am here, your steadfast lighthouse, guiding you back to calm waters.

in your eyes, i see the courage and kindness that anchors our lives.

to my husband

DAY #89

your silent battles don't go unnoticed.

i see your quiet strength, your unspoken struggles.

in those moments, know that my admiration for you only
grows.

i'm here, always, in understanding and in love.

to my husband

DAY #90

the strength you show every day doesn't have to be a solitary journey.

i'm here, your partner in every step, ready to offer a haven, a moment of peace, a comforting embrace.

to my husband

DAY *#91*

in the tapestry of our life, threads of trust and respect weave the strongest patterns.

they are the colours that make our relationship vibrant, deep, and endlessly beautiful.

to my husband

DAY *#92*

my love for you grows with each passing day.

looking ahead, i see a future filled with joy, laughter, and
endless love, all because you are in it.

to my husband

DAY #93

we've built a fortress of trust and respect, where every brick
tells a story of understanding and love.

in this sanctuary, i find the strength to be my truest self, thanks
to you.

to my husband

DAY #94

when the world gets too heavy, remember i'm right here, ready to share the weight.

your resilience inspires me, but it's your willingness to be vulnerable that truly touches my heart.

to my husband

DAY #95

as we journey through life together, i am constantly amazed at how each day with you is better than the last.

the future is ours to shape, and i can't wait to see where it takes us.

to my husband

DAY #*96*

through the years, our love has grown, not just in depth but in understanding and patience.

i cherish every memory, every lesson, and every joy we've shared.

to my husband

DAY #97

your kindness knows no bounds.

you have this unique ability to uplift and support those around
you, making each person feel valued and important.

the world needs more people like you.

to my husband

DAY #*98*

with you, i've found a love so pure and so strong, it feels like it
can weather any storm.

you're my safe harbour in this wild sea of life.

to my husband

DAY #99

every time you laugh, i fall in love all over again.

your smile lights up my world and reminds me of all the joy
we've shared.

you are my sunshine on a cloudy day.

to my husband

DAY *#100*

the sound of your laughter is the music that fills our home with
warmth and love.

your joy has become the heartbeat of our life together.

Made in the USA
Coppell, TX
15 October 2024

38698547R00059